AF265609

Two Lines
And A Garden

Words Mike Johnson

Two Lines
And A Garden

Drawings Leila Lees

99% Press

Published by 99% Press,
an imprint of Lasavia Publishing Ltd.
Auckland, New Zealand
www.lasaviapublishing.com

ISBN: 978-0-473-41-589-1

Acknowledgement

A special thanks to Daniela Gast for her subtle
arrangement of words and image.

# Part One

in the deepest forest

a dead bird calls

wakes the fitful sleeper from his dreams

cool wind blowing
a bird in mid flight
the sound of forgotten footsteps

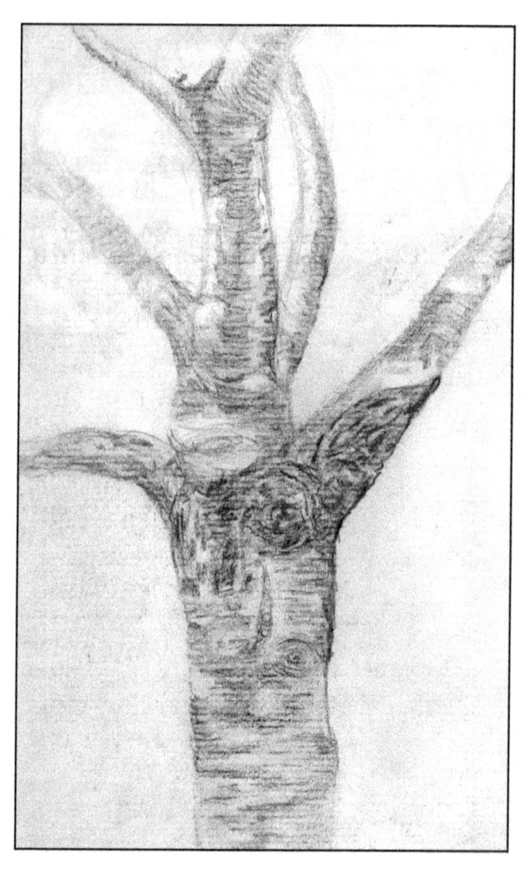

the welcome mat at the door
the windows made perfect from polishing
across the threshold, the hesitant traveller's footfall

I'm happy to be back in the world
alive and held in wonderment
beyond the tide line, no sign of life

after everything,
I still want to write love songs
and hear the tides of rain on the aluminium roof

that's me you can see dressed in woollens
I'm out there, blowing around in the wind
I'm in no hurry to arrive

it's a long way back from the edge
the morepork cries once and falls silent
the voice of a friend is sweet to the ear

I've come in from the cold and now it's warm
grief comes in a flood after a landfall
the wind makes shapes out of rain

I wouldn't want death to become too familiar

a regular visitor, as it were

we're a bit house proud around here

you may live a thousand times but only die once
once is all it takes
take a good long look at everything

you came close enough to frighten me
I started to see ghastly faces at the window
and hear the laughter of children far off

I'm too grateful to get overly complacent
like the fat kereru on his daily rounds
sleep, and I fall out of the air

in case we have forgotten, tui calls
yarb-yarb-bard-yodel-cool
hear this sigh of relief

when my back was turned, fairies ran riot
when my eyes were closed, angels danced on my face
when my heart gave up, the lucid blood went dark

I had to learn how to stand up all over again
how to keep my head in the air
now my love's teaching me how to walk

at this tender hour, dawn is just a dream

speculation in the dark

no different from a memory

you are a steady light in the unsteady night
a place for mind to feel a touch of something
and remember a garden

on the road again with you before and behind
the sound of your footfall keeps me walking
even when there's no breath left in my chest

you are there, inside your smile, unmistakable
your laughter quickly ascends to heaven
your touch, like a feather on a feather

if it weren't for your eyes, I couldn't see
if it weren't for your lips, I couldn't talk
without your grace, I couldn't take a breath

I know you're tracking me in your thoughts
sometimes I see you in your dreams, and
every time you are looking my way

every step of the way you were behind me
with your death mask on
I stopped short of turning around and looking

there comes a point when nothing else matters
except you, standing at the gate
looking back towards the house with the open windows

ah! who washed their mouth out with sunshine?
who scolded them with voice sublime?
in their extremity, who did they reach out to?

a nikau frond falls with a great crash
I wake up and stare out at the sudden wilderness
just a few bright stars on a moonless night

I've got my teaspoon of late afternoon light
I've got my bowl of night
soon, I will have my fill of a new morning

the wind turns, the temperature drops
the hawk gets blown about
a stack of firewood by the grate

I like to stay in touch with nature, but
it's all very well for me, here where the wood pigeon
unfolds the sky and scoops our valley up in its wings

I can open my door to a rough night

I can let the morepork's cry right into the house

I can shut the book and put it away at any time

the moon lies upside down, its bowl to the stars
there is a brief, welcome cold
everything with any sense is asleep

like the poet, I took up residence here on earth
looking back, probably a silly thing to do
I was better off among the aeries of my home

at 3 a.m. there is little to do but cultivate silence
perhaps the clock slows in the wee small hours
perhaps not

if I listen hard enough, I can hear the song

the round robin of the hills, the descant of the sky

the back-beat of the bamboo

where paths fork, I lie down and weep
only slowly do trees part with their wisdom
with my sharp knife, I carve initials in the air

the moon holds its place in the sky without fuss
and is still there when the clouds move on
still there after dying and coming back to life

crossing the stream, I get my feet wet, shoes and all
for a moment it's like skating on ice
I wring out my socks and wait

the lake at night is all black and silver
nothing but surface, and the depths
unimagined

the road winds uphill towards the mountains
the air crisp and sharp in the morning light
the sky gets a polish

there's a gap in the mountains where the lake extends
from the ridgelines either side, hanging valleys
and a white line where the moon joins the water

when climbing, one slope leads to another
turn around, everything looks the same
only birds are free in the trackless air

the rosella leaves behind a streak of colour
the grey ghost appears behind the curtain
and booms of times past and yet to come

shadows thread through the mountains
a line of bright water pushes the dark before it
the lake, they say, is deeper than art can tell

it seems the lake is fed directly from the sky
and is deeper than memory can tell
sloping abruptly from a tiny pebbled shore

the mist holds to the mountain like a scarf
the mountain rises to meet the clouds
as the land falls away

like the blossoms fall to a cool wind
like the stars make hollow the night sky
like the crystalline interior of a snowflake

there was a moment, the mountains grew tall
the lake shone like amethyst
black rocks gleamed

I wake in the morning beside my love
nothing could feel nicer
the world makes itself for light

the sky doesn't dither, but it might hesitate
just before dawn, it might think twice
about inviting all that light to spread everywhere

this is marmite on toast, this is a boiled egg
this is the aroma of fresh coffee
and this is a fresh span of sunlight

I like a blue that stays blue and a green that stays green
I like a yellow that moves and a violet that doesn't
I prefer the rainbows you can see on a clear day

I've seen the water shimmy on the lake
seen the eels that slither in the depths
felt the wind slip under my collar

I've heard the mountains pacing the night sky
heard the cry of extinct birds
seen the wheels of stardust turning

I've felt the touch of her on my skin
I've felt the night, and the oppression of night
tasted sunlight on sprigs of honeydew

I've smelled the nine worlds on fire
I've seen the insect struggle in the wine
enjoyed the majestic turn of her tragedy

the children are playing hopscotch on the footpath
the newly dead dream of embraces
couples stroll in and out of frame

here there are white flowers no bigger than a fingernail
as modest as modesty is
and almost as old as the world

up the river down on a great shining raft
the cosmos turns and keeps on turning
I try to do the same

we could go on like this into the dawn
break out the guitars, play some ragtime
outwait the world

as we pass this bit of garden we bow our heads
here was an act of faith and good intention
even the stones learned to sing

buds on the apricot tree are an act of hope
the blossoms are a surrender
the fruit nourishes the stone

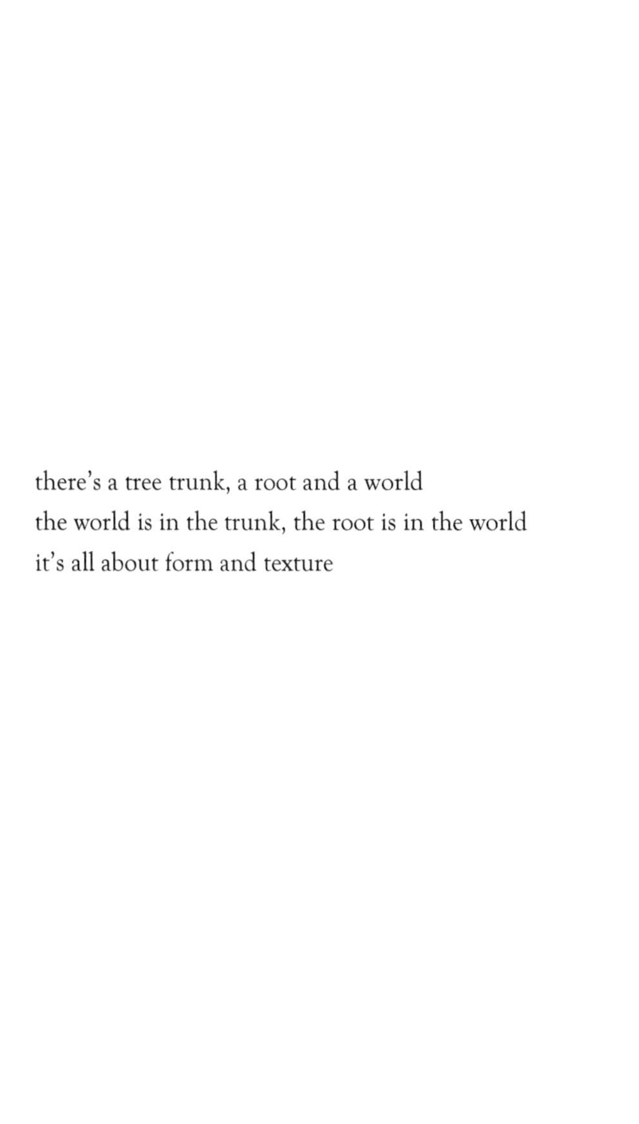

there's a tree trunk, a root and a world
the world is in the trunk, the root is in the world
it's all about form and texture

yellow leaves from the whitey-wood cover the path
it can look very festive, in the right light
with the blackbird swooping low

the westerly chases blue ghosts across the bay
a few yachts dip and bob
at the high tide mark, a man walks his dog

dawn, and the road is darker than the sky
I can walk my way by the feel of it
looking up at the stars as I go

I floated the memory down time
in a leaf-&-stick boat a child might make
to carry me to the ocean

Motokorua
o'clock ferry to waiheke
fish shades

I'm alive with a heart
left ventricle, right ventricle, an open and shut case
I haven´t skipped a beat

love and sleeplessness
walk hand and hand under a moonless night
pause, by the sound of running water

bell
birds
nesting
in
this
tree

here by the sea, I dream of the mountains
long cool icy slopes in the orange dawn
and the stiff whisper of the mountain beech

I love to seek out fast running streams
stare at the passing parade
sit and think of nothing

in the middle of the dark, off the track,
I found a wrought iron gate still attached to a post
opening to nowhere, closing on forget-me-nots

we don't talk so much about unseen things
company on the road is peppermints and a glovebox
we stop by a waterfall for packed sandwiches

we sit at a park bench and snack on nuts and raisins
tourists go past carrying chilly bins to the lake
children scream, amazed how small their voices are

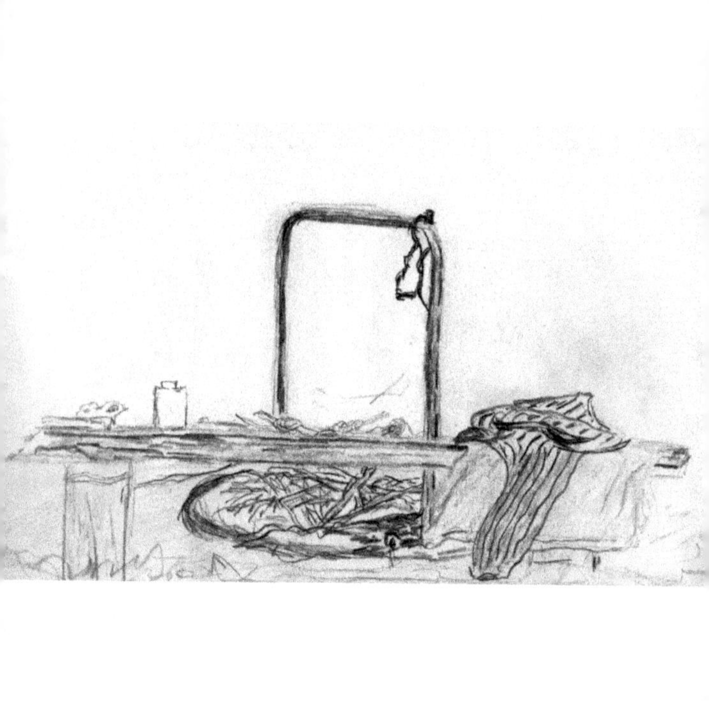

the sunset's smeared all over everything
the picnic's overthrown by baskets full of ants
a yappy dog barks itself silly

come evening, we light a fire in our valley
it gets light as it gets dark
somebody remembers the lyrics

it all goes up in the blue drift
impossible infinities breed in the tightest string
stars blink at each other across time

Part Two

our most respected scientist urges us to find another planet

such a pity!

we were just getting to know this one

they're getting rid of the witnesses
they're closing down the stations
they're chopping off their own arms and legs

it is the hour of the bird and the shadow
of regrets, griefs and farewells – tell them
sorry we couldn't find another planet in time

the nights are too warm, the rain is too hard
and the dries are too dry
but the writing on the wall's been redacted

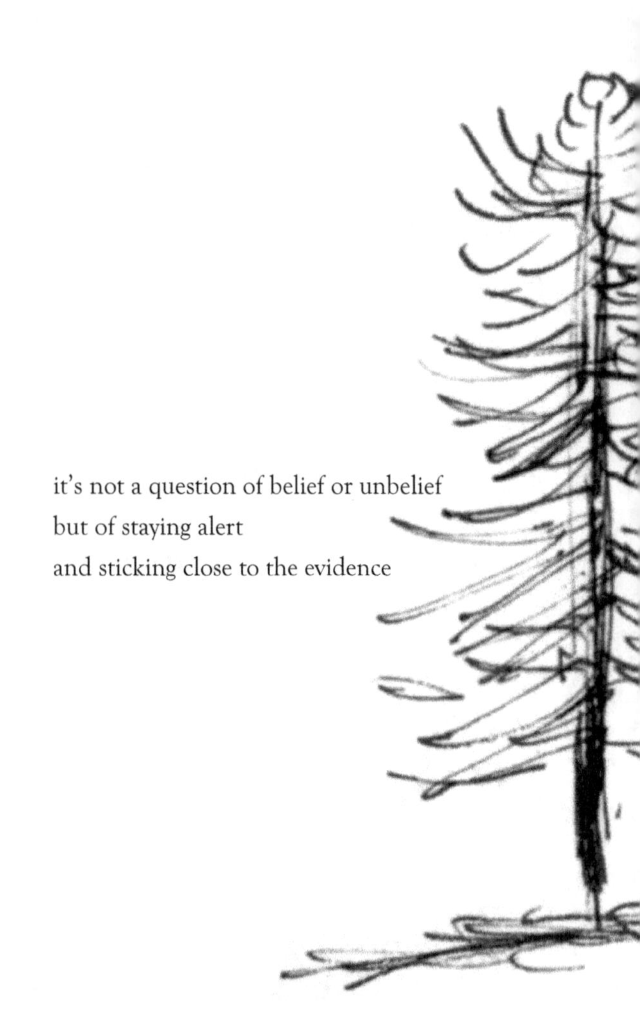

it's not a question of belief or unbelief
but of staying alert
and sticking close to the evidence

the destroyers walk among us, rich and proud
too stupid to feel shame
at the funeral, they dream of sandwiches

the sounds you hear are not of this world
they are leaking through from another dimension
someone has walked over your grave

the cold comes, the heat goes on, the rhetoric cranks up
the sky cracks open all that yellow stuff
and everybody falls into praying mode

keep a poker face as the cards fall
did fate ordain that particular hedgehog to a squashy end?
it's the Fool who plays the Joker

'you pays your money and you takes your chance,' they said
nowadays you just pays your money
and your chances are hardly worth taking

I'd love to be in tune with the great cosmic spirit
to float around in the palm of bliss
and ride the parabolic curve subline

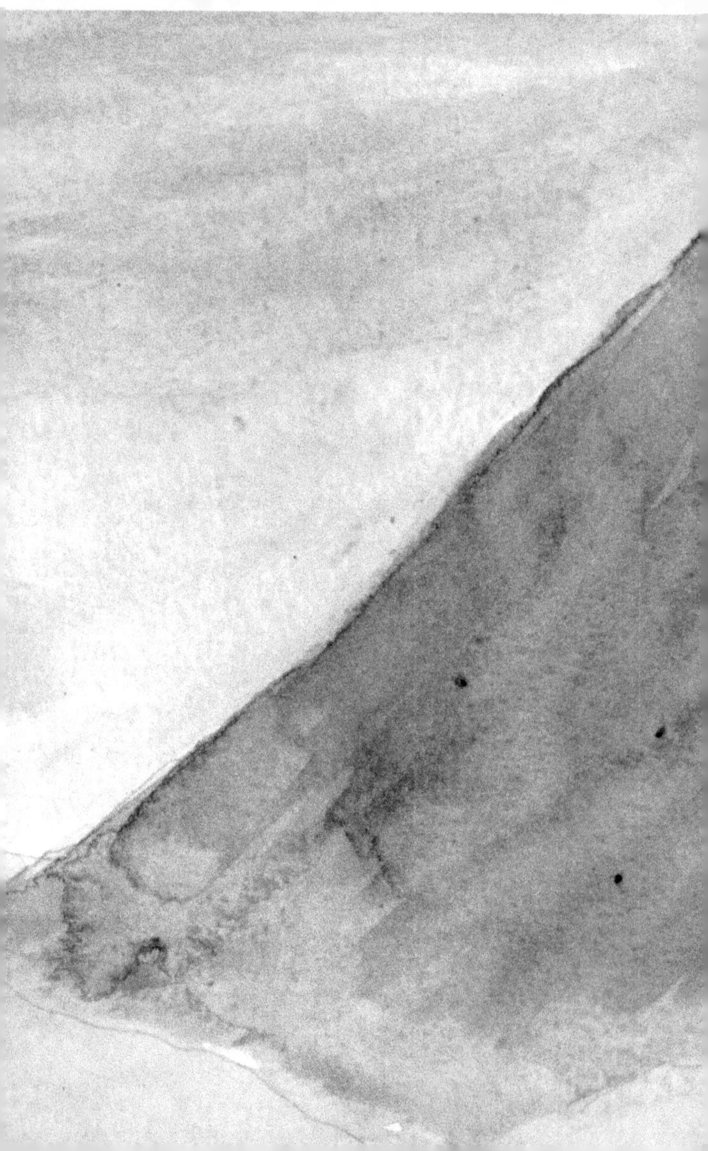

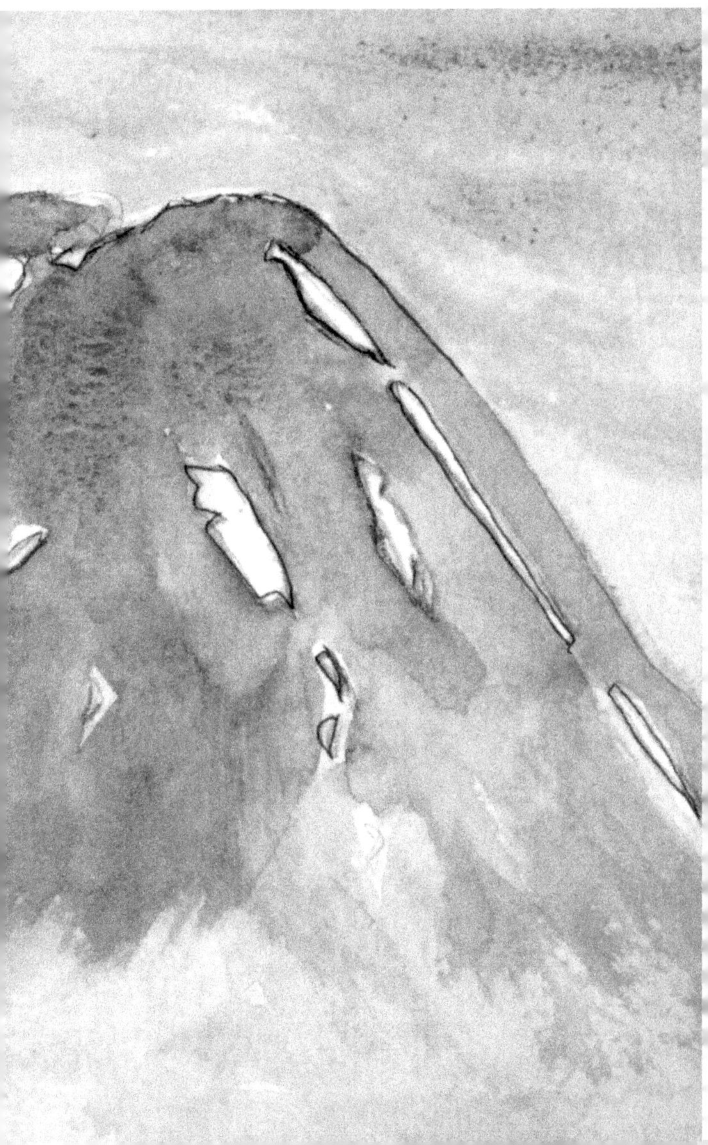

I have a book but don't read it
I have a life but don't live it
I have time and just spend it

call it a precaution, an inoculation of stardust
you can hear the music that informs our lives
taste the fever that creeps up on the dream

for the fish, no notion of rain
for the birds, no sharp stars
in the houses, no troubling gods

I am like this because you made me like this
mere clay in your hands
this shape I wear is yours, hardly mine

I think I began even before the Big Bang
universes span thumb and forefinger
between life and death float specks of dust

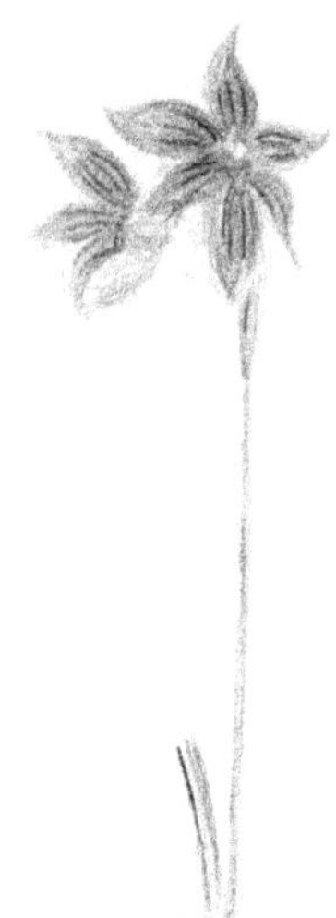

nobody here has got one up on the universe, not yet
the ace is still in the hole
it's double or nothing, gentlemen

don't get rattled when time slows, or bends back in
upon itself – time was created so that everything
doesn't happen at once, that's all

the elephant's been in the room for a long time
drinks are still being served
the elephant in the room has become part of the wallpaper

it doesn't really matter who's in charge because

no one's in charge

it actually works out better that way

we had general agreement that all was well
and would be well into the foreseeable future
at which point we ran out of beer

there are no relative directions in deep space
memory claws at time
suns explode and fizzle like firecrackers

I don't want to think about
the things
I don't want to think about

it was a quick death and a painless one, they
said
I don't know about that
words are easy

I love this island life of mine
sea and sky in every direction
words that fit, just

a full belly and a warm heart
fire in the grate
soft sheets for my love!

PART 3

you and I have such a great understanding
you take that line, I take this
they meet in the middle of the air

these days, I have to walk backwards into my words
the forward approach scares everything off
only by stealth can I knock the sparrow of its perch

language is never at rest
the time is never right
the word, one step behind, another

mountain, beach, and valley, sky and stone
these are conversations of our art
in the garden, snails come and go

turn our eyes to the heavens
or cast them down to the ground –
the horizon is that long bright line in the middle

for a while, I hought you had gone
the night was so empty, the stars so cold
the last line so far off

here're the syllables of wakefulness
the morphemes of pain, joy, and the rest of it
while the sentence has already been carried out

I've been here before, where the track falters –
a kind snake has eaten all the illness from my insides
I have to make a third line for myself

somebody sends their best wishes
somebody else remains silent
the world doesn't miss a beat

I've always looked outside myself for the next line
tears turn to beggars
when the plate of love is clean

I watch the tui drink nectar from the flax
and think only of poetry
lines of sight, samples of sound

what you see is the inscape of a branch
the intention of a leaf
the journey home

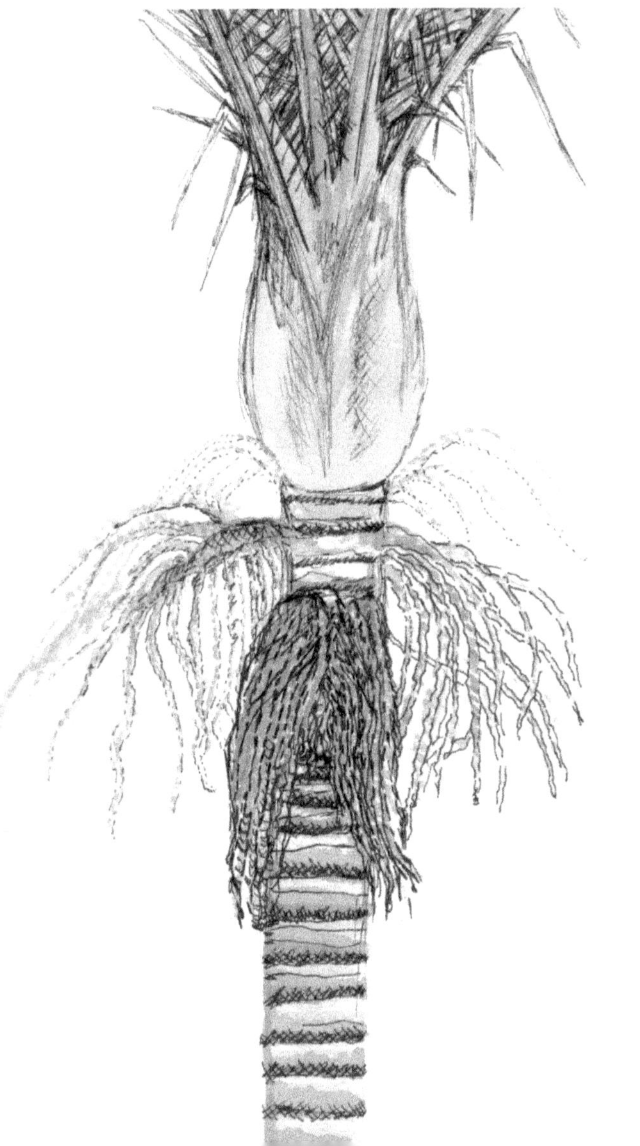

the way things are, you get three for the price of one
when you don't even need one
dead things accumulate in your blood

don't know who you are or where you've been
It all looks so settled once it's written down
looks as if it were meant to be

I've learned from the way you always sketch from nature
you hold the curve of a branch this way
and the pull of the root that

three lines is hardly enough to say anything
let alone everything, let alone the truth
or anything more than the less that shows

we've had our two lines and a garden
our cocktail hour 'neath the gauzy moon
even the shadows have grown shadows

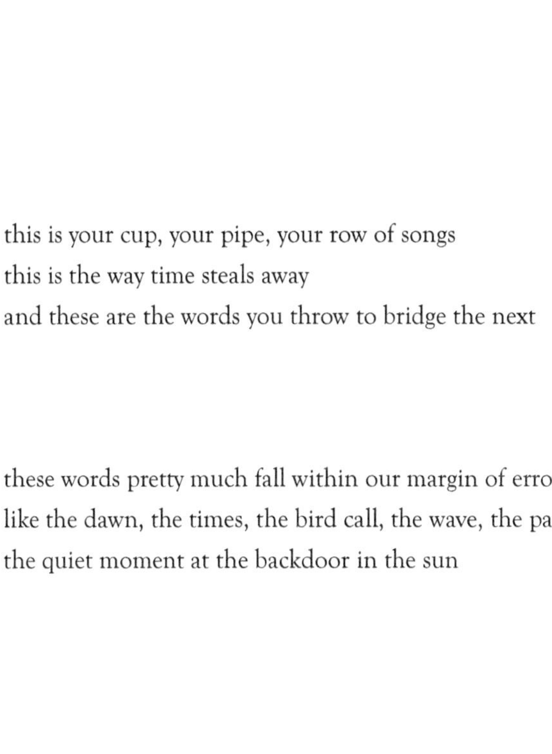

this is your cup, your pipe, your row of songs
this is the way time steals away
and these are the words you throw to bridge the next

these words pretty much fall within our margin of error
like the dawn, the times, the bird call, the wave, the page
the quiet moment at the backdoor in the sun

the dark is not really dark, but the light
takes itself quite seriously
I put down the pen, then put down the pen

www.ingramcontent.com/pod-product-compliance
Lightning Source LLC
Chambersburg PA
CBHW052356060726
47592CB00020B/2680